Richard Burton

Memorial Day and Other Poems

Richard Burton

Memorial Day and Other Poems

ISBN/EAN: 9783744710824

Printed in Europe, USA, Canada, Australia, Japan

Cover: Foto ©Thomas Meinert / pixelio.de

More available books at **www.hansebooks.com**

MEMORIAL DAY

And Other Poems

RICHARD BURTON

BOSTON
COPELAND AND DAY
M DCCC XCVII

Contents

THE POET

HE'S not alone an artist weak and white
O'er-bending scented paper, toying there
    With languid fancies fashioned deft and
      fair,
    Mere sops to time between the day and
      night.
He is a poor torn soul who sees aright
    How far he fails of living out the rare
    Night-visions God vouchsafes along the air;
    Until the pain burns hot, beyond his might.

The heart-beat of the universal will
    He hears, and, spite of blindness and dis-
      proof,
    Can sense amidst the jar a singing fine.
Grief-smitten that his lyre should lack the skill
    To speak it plain, he plays in paths aloof,
    And knows the trend is starward, life divine.

MEMORIAL DAY

" By their great memories the Gods are known."
GEO. MEREDITH.

I.

MAY is the firstling of the summer year,
  Bland month and beautiful beneath the sky ;
An Elim where the water-wells are clear,
When winter's bitter Marah is gone by.
May faces toward the pleasance yet to be,
The greenwood splendors, the maturity
Of bloom, — Hope's home is May — and May
  is here.

What semblance flashes so divinely clear
Yet mystic to the dazzled eye as this
Of Hope ? Not Youth alone, but manhood's
  cheer,
Old age's desolation, sorrow's kiss
Above a tomb, — these all draw strength from
  her,
Quenchless, the first, the final comforter,
What Being utterly shall of her miss ?

But kinsman proper unto Hope, the bright,
Is Memory, elder, graver, wrapt in Time
As in a mantle : mellow is the light
She casts, obliquely : images sublime
She conjures up, and barren were the days
That missed the magic of her holy haze,
Making old seasons seem a summer clime.

I

Yea, not in Hope alone are mortals strong :
They have their memories ; looking down the
    past,
We do behold them, a most stately throng
Of figures in a mould heroic cast :
Recumbent, but all vital to arouse
A nation, and to quicken a people's vows
By proud ensample of the lives that last.

If by their memories the Gods are known,
So too are men and women, for they grow
God-like in telling over all their own
Emblazoned deeds ; heroes are nourished so,
Idealisms spring, romances thrive
Wherever those with heart and hope alive
Draw solace from the great of long ago.

Moved by this sense of dignity inurned
In scenes historic and in moments great,
Heart-touched by tender thoughts of knighthood
    earned
On scarlet fields, each hero-mindful state
Gathers around the graves of fallen sons,
And covers up the flesh-scars and the guns
With flowers, those soft effacers of old hate.

II.

May and the sunshine keen on everything !
But hark ! the martial music's solemn sound :
Now, in the forefront of the plastic spring,
Pause momently, and let the ancient wound
Quiver again, — not for dark rancour's sake,

2

But only forever to keep wide awake
Memories of deaths superb and courage-crowned.

Now is the cleavage deep of North and South
Well closed, — the years o'er-cover it, as grass
Softens and sweetens some dry place of drouth
When comes the blessed rain ; the requiem-mass
Is chanted of the mood that shattered peace :
Where common sorrows are, anger must cease :
Sorrow and love remain, while passions pass.

And if there come wild words of East and West,
Let us invoke our mighty memories
Even as the Gods again ; declare it best
To sail together over tranquil seas,
One ship, one helmsman, one ambition high :
To show the world a strength that can lay by
War, and the thought of war, and such as these.

Yea, mingle prayers above the Blue and Gray,
And be the pæans raised for patriot sires
Who in that hour of Freedom's yesterday
Fought sturdily, and lit their beacon fires
For what they deemed the Right.   The victor
   shows
Himself twice victor when his sometime foes
Are hailed as brothers, even as Christ requires.

How like cathedral chimes the names we know,
Ringing above a leal united land :
Bull Run, Antietam, Gettysburg, Shiloh,
Sherman's grim march to reach the white sea-strand,

3

Lookout's cloud fight, The Wilderness, — each bell
Reverberating valor — list! they tell
How Lincoln and Lee are friends, and under-
stand.

III.

What is a patriot?   Not the man who swears:
"My country, right or wrong;" nor he who
claims
That sacred thing, yet like a dastard dares
To use her to his ends, to hide his shames;
Nor yet the weakling sore afraid to chide
For fear he seem untrue: the gap is wide
'Twixt empty mouthings and high manhood's
aims.

A patriot?   He should be a blend of faith
And fealty and fear of any stain
Upon his mistress' honor; for the wraith
Of mere Appearance many a man hath slain,
Who reckoned that blind praise was Duty's all.
Who loves, chastises; at his country's call,
Behold him valiant in the van again!

He agonizes o'er the awful plight
Of that disfeatured host that lacks for bread;
He watches Labor in her new-found might
Strike at Monopoly's dire dragon head;
He lets the Time-spirit lead him towards the
truth,
That mind see clear and heart be moved to ruth
For the land's children who are sore-bested.

4

O Country! vast, — dramatic, thrilled with life, *Memorial Day.*
O mother! bountiful of womb and breast,
We may reproach thee, even use the knife
For pain's release upon thy body, lest
Fair growth be checked, — but should an alien
  dare
Befoul thy fame, a lion from its lair
Each state shall spring, each burg prove loyalest.

Into thy sinews enter Norse and Celt,
The German and the Gaul, they westward steer :
From the frore north and from the southern belt
Of nations come the folk to fellow here :
But under-bone is English, sturdy stock,
Pliant to Fate, yet founded like a rock :
Fraternal, all, in Freedom's atmosphere !

For higher, holier than the will to war
The will to love, — now may the path of Peace
Within our states be like the pilot star
In the night sky, by myriads to increase
As the millennium broadens, gleam by gleam :
This is the prophet's word, the poet's dream :
All nations living in love's great release.

Call not this womanish, a sluggard's hope :
When whilom brave men lay their swords aside,
They still are brave : but they no longer grope
In the earth-chambers where the beasts abide,
But, feet firm-based, they lift their foreheads high
Into the ample air, and from the sky
Draw loftier inspirations, larger-eyed.

5

Memorial Day. Nay, on this day memorial ne'er forget
The visioned good, the revelation august
Of Peace betwixt the peoples : may we let
Our martial blood be cleansed of any lust
Of war, and this America clasp hands
Close with the parent English, two proud lands
Before the world who let their weapons rust.

Memories and hopes !   O mingle on this day
Savored with flowers, made sacred by the tears
Of mourners, musical with the far-away
Sound of large doings from the vanished years ;
And buoyant, midst the muséd tenderness,
Through the stanch creed that, slowly, Wrong
  grows less,
The while our land, God guided, hath no fears!

MATTERHORN QUESTS

AS men essay the Matterhorn —
  That peering peak of stone and snow —
To view, some matchless Alpine morn,
  The petty world stretch far below,
Though after all their toil and pain
  They can but clamber down again ;

So yearning souls essay the heights
  Of spirit, setting dangers by,
And recking naught of low delights
  The flesh affords ; you ask them why,
They know not ; some divine unrest
  Bids them to climb and do their best.

6

IN TIME OF BATTLE

IT is a seemly thing to die in battle,
  Ensanguined for the Right ;
The sudden swoon, the ominous death-rattle,
    Mere phantoms in the fight
Against the music and the Victor's cry ;
    'Tis noble so to die.

And if one fail, 'tis well in such disaster
    Like Saul to end the day ;
Philistine spears fly fast and blood flows faster,
    The leader falls, but they,
His dauntless sons, fall with him, all the three
    Under a tamarisk tree
In Jabesh !   And it is a fate full splendid
    To win a funeral song
Like David's, love and leonine sorrow blended
    All passionate and strong ;
The King made moan for Saul, his Mighty One ;
    But most for Jonathan.

A FAITHFUL DOG

MY merry-hearted comrade on a day
  Gave over all his mirth, and went away
Upon the darksome journey I must face
Sometime as well.   Each hour I miss his grace,
His meek obedience and his constancy.
Never again will he look up to me
With loyal eyes, nor leap for my caress
As one who wished not to be masterless ;
And never shall I hear his pleading bark

7

A Faithful Dog. Outside the door, when all the ways grow dark,
Bidding the house-folk gather close inside.
It seems a cruel thing, since he has died,
To make his memory small, or deem it sin
To reckon such a mate as less than kin.

O faithful follower, O gentle friend,
If thou art missing at the journey's end,
Whate'er of joy or solace there I find
Unshared by thee I left so far behind,
The gladness will be mixed with tears, I trow,
My little crony of the long ago !
For how could heaven be home-like, with the
    door
Fast-locked against a loved one, evermore ?

SO MUCH TO LEARN

SO much to learn !   Old Nature's ways
Of glee and gloom with rapt amaze
To study, probe, and paint, — brown earth,
Salt sea, blue heavens, their tilth and dearth,
Birds, grasses, trees, — the natural things
That throb or grope or poise on wings.

So much to learn about the world
Of men and women !   We are hurled
Through interstellar space awhile
Together, then the sob, the smile,
Is silenced, and the solemn spheres
Whirl lonesomely along the years.

8

So much to learn from wisdom's store
Of early art and ancient lore.
So many stories treasured long
On temples, tombs, and columns strong.
The legend of old eld, so large
And eloquent from marge to marge.

So much to learn about one's self:
The fickle soul, the nimble elf
That masks as me ; the shifty will,
The sudden valor and the thrill ;
The shattered shaft, the broken force
That seems supernal in its source.

And yet the days are brief.   The sky
Shuts down before the waking eye
Has bid good-morrow to the sun ;
The light drops low, and Life is done.
Good-by, good-night, the star-lamps burn ;
So brief the time, so much to learn !

THE LITTLE MOTHERS

STRANGE mockery of motherhood !
They who should feel the fostering care
Maternal, and the tender good
   Of home when fondling arms are there,

Must, ere their time, in mimic show
   Of age and sacred duties, be
Thus wise to guide, thus deep to know,
   The artless needs of infancy.

9

The little mothers !　Will they win
　　The bitter-sweet of elder years ?
Will love protect them from the sin,
　　And faith gleam dauntless through the tears ?

God grant some guerdon for the loss
　　Of childly joy : and when they come
To woman-ways and woman's cross,
　　Give them a fate more frolicsome.

THE PROLOGUE

Scene, a theatre. The audience is crowding
　　its way in ; the play is Dekker's " The
　　Pleasant Comedy of Old Fortunatus."

1st Spectator.

HEY ! how they push !　The pit is crowded
　　now ;
A family man must come in season, sooth,
If he would see the play.　On Saturdays
The folk, work finished, bring their wives and all,
Hoarding each penny through the thrifty week.
And look ! an actor comes, 'tis curtain-time.

　　2d Spec.　Nay, 'tis but Master Prologue, he
　　　　that struts
About the stage and mouths to please himself,
Speedily making way for the real stuff,
The kings and queens and all the quality
That sit at banquet in the regal hall.

　　3d Spec.　Thou liest, fool, see where they
　　　　pantomime ;
There's more than one ; faith, 'tis the very play.

10

2d Spec.   God's love, it is a zany.   Proper The
  plays
Have each their fore-piece ; so it is to-day.

1st Spec.'s Wife.   Peace, dolt !   They speak ;
  only the gallants talk,
The yeomanry should hearken, look and learn.
            [*The play begins without a prologue.*

1st Cobbler in audience.   How handsomely
  they give the lines.   Methinks
There never was a scene since I was got
So brave in carriage, nor by half so grand,
As this of Fortunatus and his purse.
'Twas well for him he chose the chink of gold
Afore aught else — as, wisdom, beauty, health.

2d Cob.   I heard but now good Master
  Prentice there
(Him yonder with his dame) affirm it roundly
That he had sometime seen this famous piece,
And how these incidents are all aside
From the grave acts that make the tragedy,
The true main action that will come erelong ;
This a mere farce to make us laugh withal.
I trow he has it right.

1st Cob.   Th'art drunken, man ;
The actors sweat as though 'twas serious ;
And mark you that the stage is gallant-full,
Which would not be unless the act's begun.

11

3*d Cob.* Yet, by my awl, 'tis hardly six o'
    the clock,
And he says true, the fore-piece comes the first ;
Mayhap it is new-fangled, Spanish, French,
To speak the prologue by more mouths than one.
Nay, Hodge is right, 'tis surely not the play.

2*d Cob.* Ye silly knaves, I prithee prate no
    more ;
I know the playhouse, and if this be not
The prologue, nothing else, I'll buy and burn
Ten tapers for the church come Candlemas.
    [*The play is enacted, and, being finished,
      the people jostle their way out of the pit.*

1*st Citizen.* 'Twas handsome-done, — but
    still a parlous trick,
This giving of the plot with ne'er a word
Of fore-speech, when one looked for something
    such ;
Though I have heard it said 'tis often so,
This showing of the play sans anything
To gloss it. Well, I would that I had known ;
So would I not have chattered with my mates,
Thinking the best to come, but bent my mind
On Fortunatus and his fortunes great.
I lost full half the lines, by our lady, yes.
'Twould fetch the tears another time. Ah me,
Had I but known ! A play's a mocking thing !

So is it with us men. We watch the stage,
And cannot deem that what is playing there

(Bespite the fuss and fustian and the roars
Of laughter that Sir Cap-and-Bells provokes)
Is still the one brief tragedy that we
Spectators ere shall gaze on ; that the time
Is only hours few, — one afternoon
Snatched from a grim eternity of days.
Secure in a false ease and thinking, fond,
How 'tis the fore-piece that but ushers in
The five-act story, — lo ! our life is lived ;
The lights go down, and we, half blinking still,
Must elbow out into the night and cold,
Uncertain whether, as we stumble on,
Of all the friendly press whose smiles and tears
Made company about us just before,
One voice shall hail us, or a fellow hand
Stretch forth to touch us in the silent dark.

THE OLD TENOR

A MONOLOGUE

DID you say the singing was only fair ?
Sir, if the chance was given me
To change from him on the stage up there
　　Straight to a spirit symphony —

Well, it might stagger my poor old brain,
　　But I think, on the whole, I back should come
To hear these worn sweet notes again,
　　And see yon form that is cumbersome.

The why of it all ?　It fell, my friend,
　　A matter of forty years ago.

13

A certain man was nigh his end,
    Lying wracked in a fever glow,

And a fine young star, in his flush of fame,
    Stept to his bedside, took his hand,
And strove to kindle life's spent flame
    By singing songs of the lovely land.

Ah, how he sang ! till the sick man turned
    His face from the wall, and took deep breath,
And said, as his eyes with new light yearned,
    That life ran sweeter far than death

If one might hearken to strains like this ;
    And he swore he would live in death's despite.
Then sleep dropt down on him like a kiss,
    And he woke with his blood all cool and right.

Perhaps you can fancy who was the man,
    And who is the singer there on the stage,
And why I listen and sob, and can
    But love his faults and his hints of age.

Some folks will say, when they pay their coin,
    The perfectest singer is their choice,
Where youth and art and genius join ;
    But I like a *man* behind the voice !

THE PHANTOM DRUM

A LEGEND OF CASTINE

THE old fort stands on the sightly hill
　Engirt by bays and the wide salt sea ;
Its earthworks soft with the grass a-grow
And the gold of flowers, its bastions low.
How tranquil Time doth work his will
On the stormy heights of history !

Of yore the British ensconced them here,
Old battle dogs in their rig of red ;
But the Yankees came, and who might cope
With the men afire with freedom's hope ?
A vanquished foe, with a victor's cheer
At their very heels, the red-coats fled.

In a pit deep dug in mother earth,
In a transient prison nigh the wall,
Left behind was a drummer lad ;
Clean forgotten him they had,
And his petty fault and his ways of mirth ;
No comrade stayed for to heed his call.

Buried alive there, he and his drum !
Tireless he beat it, a reveille
Would wake the dead, but no living wight
Was near to succor by day or night ;
He prayed that even the foe might come
Before he had starved himself away.

In vain : when the patriot band marched there
In after days, and the rampart scaled,
They found his drum-head broken through
With the hapless blows, and the drummer too
Life-spent ; what once was strong and fair
Shrunk to a thing whereat men paled.

    .   .   .   .

'Twas in March it fell : a century's tide
Flows full between ; but the legend claims,
Whenever the windy month comes round,
You shall hear by night as doleful sound
As ever rose o'er the ocean wide
Or frightened the children at their games.

'Tis the phantom drum's tap-tapping drear
Up in the fort ; for he cannot rest,
That drummer boy in his dungeon place ;
You never see him or know his face,
But the tap-tap-tap comes sharp and clear
Above the sea, when the wind blows west.

THE RACE OF THE "BOOMERS"

THE bleak o' the dawn, and the plain is a-
smoke with the breath of the frost,
And the murmur of bearded men is an ominous
sound in the ear ;
The white tents liken the ground to a flower-
meadow embossed
By the bloom of the daisy sweet, for a sign
that the June is here.

They are faring from countless camps, afoot or
    ahorse, may be,
    The blood of many a folk may flow in their
    bounding veins,
But, stung by the age-old lust for land and for
    liberty,
    They have ridden or run or rolled in the mile-
    engulfing trains.

More than the love of loot, mightier than wom-
    an's lure,
    The passion that speeds them on, the hope
    that is in their breast :
They think to possess the soil, to have and to
    hold it sure,
    To make it give forth of fruit in this garden
    wide of the West.

But see ! It is sun-up now, and six hours hence
    is noon ;
    The crowd grows thick as the dust that muffles
    the roads this way :
The black-leg stays from his cards, the song-man
    ceases his tune,
    And the gray-haired parson deems it is idle to
    preach and pray.

Now thirst is a present pain and hunger a coming
    dread,
    Water is dear as gold, as the heat grows fierce
    apace :

Theft is a common deed for the price of a bit of
     bread,
  And poison has played its part to sully the
  morning's face.

And over the mete away the prairie is parched
     and dry,
  A creature of mighty moods, an ocean of move-
  less waves ;
Clean of a single soul, silent beneath the sky,
  Waiting its peopled towns, with room for a
  host of graves.

The hours reel on, and tense as a bow-cord
     drawn full taut
  Is the thought of the Boomers all : a sight that
  is touched with awe ;
A huddle of men and horse to the frenzy pitch
     upwrought,
  A welter of human-kind in the viewless grip of
  the Law.

Lo ! women are in the press, by scores they are
     yonder come
  To find a footing in front — ah, how can they
  gain a place ?
Nay, softly, even here in the rabble are harbored
     some
  Who think of their mothers, wives, who re-
  member a fairer face ;

For the black mass yawns to let these weak ones
 into the line,
 While as many men fall back : 'tis knighthood
  nameless and great,
Since it means good-by to a claim — yea, the
 end of a dream divine,
 To be lord of the land, and free for to follow a
  larger fate.

High noon : with a fusillade of guns and a deep,
 hoarse roar,
 With a panting of short, sharp breaths in the
  mad desire to win,
Over the mystic mark the seething thousands pour,
 As the zenith sun glares down on the rush and
  the demon's din.

God ! what a race : all life merged in the arrowy
 flight ;
 Trample the brother down, murder, if need
  be so,
Ride like the wind and reach the Promised Land
 ere night,
 The Strip is open, is ours, to build on, harrow
  and sow.

There comes a Horror of flame, for look, the
 grass is afire !
 On, or it licks our feet, on, or it chokes our
  breath !
Swift through the cactus fly, swift, for it kindles
 higher ;

19

Home and love and life — or the hell of an
    awful death.

So, spent and bruised and scorched, down trail
    thick-strewn with hopes
    A-wreck, did the Boomers race to the place
    they would attain ;
Seizing it, scot and lot, ringing it round with
    ropes,
    The homes they had straitly won through fire
    and blood and pain.

    .   .   .   .

While ever up from the earth, or fallen far through
    the air,
    Goes a shuddering ethnic moan, the saddest of
    all sad sounds ;
The cry of an outraged race that is driven other-
    where,
    The Indian's heart-wrung wail for his hapless
    Hunting Grounds.

BALLAD OF THE EASTERN WOMAN

(In Turner's "History of England" is told the story of a
Mahometan woman who fell in love with an English merchant, the father of Thomas à Becket, and followed him all
the way to England, although she knew but the word *London*,
and the word *Gilbert*, the name of her lover.)

IT was an eastern woman
    Who hailed from over seas,
And she met an English merchant,
    And sought his heart to please.

She met an English merchant
    All in her native land,
Who kissed her there and called her fair,
    And plighted her his hand.

But merchant men are fickle :
    Anon he took him home,
With cargo heavy-laden ;
    He would no longer roam :
He left the eastern woman
    To weep if so she would,
Nor weened to stay another day
    If but the wind held good.

The eastern woman hoarded
    What moneys to her came ;
She knew his city, London,
    She knew his Christian name,
And this was all her knowledge ;
    But with a faith sublime
She journeyed far by sun and star,
    Nor recked of tide or time.

O'er half the world she travelled
    Until (for God above
Had pity on such trusting,
    Had marvel at such love)
Unto the isle of England
    She came in her emprise,
A lonely one whose eastern sun
    Was in her hair and eyes.

21

And one bleak day the good folk
    Who thronged upon the street
Were stricken still a moment
    To see a sight full sweet :
A soft-lipped orient woman
    Repeating o'er and o'er
Her lover's name and whence he came, —
    Two words, and nothing more.

But, lo! her Gilbert passing !
    He meets her face to face
And all his heart is molten
    Before her hapless grace ;
A mighty cry she utters,
    And then looks dumbly down.
Oh, love will lead and give good speed,
    Though strange be tongue and town !

So merchant Gilbert took her,
    And swore that she was true,
And wed the eastern woman
    Ere yet the moon was new.
And she was well-requited
    For stress by land and sea,
And lived her life as glad a wife
    As ever did ladye.

BALLAD OF THE THORNLESS ROSE

A SSISI town had a garden once
With roses set of a wondrous kind.
And Francis, monk, was the gardener
(The world is still with his name astir)
  To shield them from the wind.

For they grew and blew in that peaceful spot
  With never a thorn to prick the hand
Of one that plucked them, — if but he
Loved Christ and trowed on his sovereignty,
  Or fought with a believing brand.

But there came a maid of noble race
  Once on a time to the garden fair,
And saw the monk and loved him well,
As he loved her, for she drew the spell
  Of her beauty round him there.

But she was a heathen in her faith,
  And he was a man to Mary vowed;
Yet, — fain to show her a tender sign,
He plucked a rose with a heart like wine
  And gave to this lady proud.

Whereat she took it with gracious smile,
  And knew that it meant a love untold;
Blusht and put it beside her breast
(A place, I ween, for a rose the best)
  In that garden sweet and old.

23

Then she turned away and rode her home :
    But when it was come to harvest-tide
She loved a lord of her kin and creed,
Forgot the monk and his true love deed,
    And soon was a stately bride.

And, wotting well that it shamed her truth,
    She called a vassal and bade him go
Back to the monk with the withered rose,
Back to the empty garden-close
    Wherein no flowers blow.

And lo ! when Francis unrolled the silk
    That wrapt the flower all bruised and dead,
And touched the stem, sharp thorns had grown
About the bloom of that rose alone
    Of all in his garden-bed !

Then Francis, monk, said never a word,
    But kissed the petals, and soft at night
Stole him out to a secret place
And buried the flower, and hid his face
    In prayer till the morning light.

    .   .   .   .

'Twas the woman's heathen hand, write some,
    But the peasants have it another way :
The thorns grew out of her faithless love
(The same is a sin all sins above)
    And girt the rose that day.

IRONY

A LOVER sued for his lady's hand,
   But her heart was stone, and he went his
      way
And served the flag of his native land
   And fought and wounded fell one day.

And the tidings came to his lady love
   As a sudden stroke from an open sky ;
Till she knew she held, all men above,
   Yon stricken one who was like to die.

So she rose, with the message blindly read,
   And breathed a prayer for a kindly fate ;
" I will go to him," she palely said,
   " And tell my love ere it be too late."

When she reached the field and sought for one
   To say in sooth how her hero fared,
She deemed her earthly sorrows done,
   And joyed for all she had dreamed and dared,

For the wound, they said, was healing fast
   And the doubt and danger now were o'er.
Ah, the woman's tears dropt down at last,
   While her heart kept singing more and more.

She bent above him as white he lay,
   Nor held it wanting in womanhood
To bare her soul to his gaze, and say
   The word she felt he would reckon good.

25

Irony. But a look of pain to his sick face stole
          And wonder sat on the weary brow,
      As, truth for truth, he told the whole
          Simple story of Then and Now.

      After days of a long despair
          He had found another whose eye confessed
      She held him dear, — and her lock of hair
          Nestled now on his bandaged breast.

      Then the lady rose with the story heard,
          And murmured not at the turn of fate,
      But looked to heaven and spake this word :
          " Even so, I have come too late."

MAD-TOWN

DID you ever hear of Mad-Town,
      A town I wot of well ?
How once men called it glad-town,
      And what the folk befell ?

      Of yore, the place was like to other towns,
  Where old and young and seemly men and clowns
      Lived out their lives ; and maidens smiled or
          broke
          Deep hearts, or were bespoke.
      Where tiny children sported midst the downs,
  Weaving of flowers or bringing in the May,
          Merry the live-long day,
      And matrons most demure, with upbound hair,
  Did household tasks and wept betimes for care ;

While Shrunken-shanks sat still and took their
   sunning,
     And watched the younkers running.

Until, one morn, just as the night-lorn East
   Turned into rose that wine sheds at a feast,
A stranger came, bearing an instrument
   With carvings strange besprent,
And stood and played : the lordliest and the least
   About the streets, afield, or housed at home
     Stopt, and might not roam.
Stopt, and light ran over all their faces,
   Yea, blest them in their places.
And as the minstrel, playing soft and sweet,
   Waxed loving in his work, lo ! many feet
Kept rhythmic time, and bodies swayed, and hands
     Were claspt for dancing-bands.
   And e'en the little ones, too wee to beat
The perfect dance-time through its cadences,
     Were rhythmic in their glees ;
One old man, too, albeit bent with eld,
   Rose up in raptures never to be quelled
And cast afar his staff, to hobble gayly,
     As he had done it daily.

The player played right on, tune chasing tune,
   Until the clocks rang out, high noon ! high
    noon !
Then sudden vanished, sprang into the air,
     Or sank through earth ere any were aware :
   And oh ! the change, the sorry, woeful swoon
From joyance that was rife erewhile he went

                    And ceased his blandishment !
            Each face grew stony first, then vacant-eyed,
                And gibberish loud laughter rose and died
            To silence worse, like damnéd spirits striving
                    Against their Fate's contriving.

            And though this happed full many years ago,
                And one might deem they had forgot it so,
            Forgot the minstrel and his coming-time,
                    As one forgets a rhyme :
            The good folk of the town forever show
            This strange wild grieving after what is dead
                    In what the music said.
            Until men call them mad : they neither reap
                Nor sow, nor buy nor sell, but only sleep ;
            Or, waking, roam with head aside, as trying
                    To catch some sound a-dying.

            ————

                    This is the tale of Mad-Town,
                        A town I wot of well ;
                    How once men called it glad-town,
                        And what the folk befell.

Melodies of The Months

MARCH FIELDS

NOW shrink not from me for shamefacedness,
O sober fields of March beneath the sky !
Your brown and gray, your russet robes, may
  bless
With deep delight a lover's loyal eye ;
And lover such and always fain would I
Be reckoned, who in all my blood to-day,
Long winter-sluggish, feel a mighty wine,
The wind of spring that sings along its way,
And makes a music that is festal-fine.
O sober fields of March, your mood is deep,
  divine !

APRIL

THE lyric tremor and lift
        Of the renascent earth,
        The teeming birth
Again, the indescribable gift
Of Spring, a-throb with everything
        That's wonder-worth.

Let us have eyes to see
        The new-old miracle!
        If it befell
We viewed for the first time such wizardry,
Each budding leaf were past belief,
        Ineffable.

But custom films our eyes
        Unto the marvellous sight,
        And April bright
Is not a magic-maiden from the skies,
But an earth-girl of pout and curl
        And manner light.

        Ah, no! not so :
She is God's daughter, and her airiest mood
Is deep with Love and wise with ancient
        Good.

MAY–LURE

HOW the heart pulls at its tether
    In the magic warm spring weather!
How the blood leaps in its courses
When the deep ebullient forces
Break the bosom brown of earth!

        It is worth
All a man can scrape or squander
Just to idle, just to wander
Forth from trade, away from duty,
Revelling in all the beauty
And the glamour of the May.

        Who to-day
Cares a fig for any other
Thought save this : The earth, great mother,
Has turned kind, has banished gloom and dole ;
Music, that audient outlet for the soul,
Comes in, and grief goes out, and Life is whole.

JUNE

JUNE in the grass!
Daisies and buttercups, lo, they surpass
Coined gold of kings ; and for greendom, the
rose,
Bloom of the month, see how stately she goes ;
Blow, winds, and waft me the breathings of
flowers :
June's in her bowers.

June overhead!
All the birds know it, for swift they have sped
Northward, and now they are singing like mad ;
June is full-tide for them, June makes them glad.
Hark, the bright choruses greeting the day —
Sorrow, away !

June in the heart !
Dormant dim dreamings awake and upstart,
Blood courses quicker, some sprite in my feet
Makes rhythm of motion, makes wayfaring sweet ;
So, outward or inward, the meaning is clear ;
Summer is here.

HAYING

A RUSTIC idyl of the ardent days
In middle summer. When the sun is new
The scythes go swishing all the wet grass through,
Making a music down the meadow ways ;
And as the noon draws on, in fields ablaze

Haying.   With heat, the rows are gathered trig and true,
To simmer there beneath the cloudless blue,
    And spill keen fragrance.   In the twilight haze,
Behold ! the high-piled wain along the road
    Creaks cumbrously, the hayers spent and brown
Seated a-top ; — so huge their precious load
    They brush the bushes, well-nigh topple down ;
The field stands stript ; — a gust of evening rain,
    And all its face is odorous again.

Bird Notes

THE LARK

I STOOD knee-deep within a field of grain,
And felt a sudden flash of facile wings
That off the ground rose straight into the blue.
And looking, saw it was the lark, a wight
In all my days I had not glimpsed at home,
And now must find beyond the foam-white seas
For the first time.   This child of ecstasy
Shook down roulades of song, and clove the air
Up, up and ever up towards very heaven,
A speck of buoyant life against the sky,
And bird-kind's one embodiment of soul
In God-aspiring flight.   Across my mind
Rushed Shakespeare's hymn and Shelley's heav-
enly lay,
Wherein this bird, etherealized, becomes
More beautiful, and less of mortal mould ;
Until half-dazed I stood, nor hardly knew
Whether I heard the descant of the lark,
Or those dear singers of the human race
Make subtle music for my brooding ear.

THE CAT–BIRD

A SKULKER in a thicket, loud and harsh
His note, his message so unbeautiful
It does belie his bird shape, cheat the sense.
But hark !   All suddenly a wondrous lay

33

And from the self-same throat. 'Tis now a thrush
Uttering its nunlike spirit on the air;
And now a robin, cheery-sweet and plumed
For morning minstrelsy that wakes the day;
And now a mingled rapture of them both
With Somewhat superadded. A strange bird,
Yet in his fashion not unlike to man,
Who often hides a music-potent soul
Under some uncouth semblance of a song
That strikes the ear but lamely, — till some stress
Of life, some lyric impulse, bids him break
His custom, and the world is blessedly
Enthralled, the melody is so divine.

THE MEISTERSINGER

THE magic moment of the eve has come,
When keen behind the hill the after-glow
Makes gold and flame of heaven, too soon to change
To mother-of-pearl; and hark! the hid thrush sings
His master-song, wee Walter of the wood,
So silvery and sweet that one is sure
He'll win his Eva, put to shame for aye
All rivals, prove himself a knight indeed
At minstrelsy, and live by music's might
So long as men have ears and Time a tongue.

THE HUMMING–BIRD

IS it a monster bee,
  Or is it a midget bird,
Or yet an air-born mystery
  That now yon marigold has stirred,
And now on vocal wing
  To a neighbor bloom is whirred,
In an aery ecstasy, in a passion of pilfering ?

Ah ! 'tis the humming-bird,
  Rich-coated one,
  Ruby-throated one,
That is not chosen for song,
But throws its whole rapt sprite
  Into the secrets of flowers
The summer days along,
  Into most odorous hours,
Into a murmurous sound of wings too swift for
  sight !

THE BLUEBIRD

IN the very spring,
  Nay, in the bluster of March, or haply
    before,
    The bluebird comes, and, a-wing
    Or alight, seems evermore
    For song that is sweet and soft.
        His footprints oft
    Make fretwork along the snow
    When the weather is bleak ablow,
When his hardihood by cold is pinched full sore.

Then deep in the fall,
In the Indian-summer while, in the dreamy days,
        When the errant songsters all
        Grow slack in songful ways,
        You may hear his warble still
                By field or hill ;
        Until, with an azure rush
        Of motion, music — hush !
He is off, he is mutely whelmed in the southern
    haze !

THE GROUND–ROBIN

FROM a low birch-tree just outside my win-
    dow,
Here in the wind-fresh green New Hampshire
    country,
All through the day, and even at the nightfall,
Cheery, distinct, his heart a home for hope,
His throat full swollen with desire of music,
A little ground-robin sits and sings,
Symbol of summer, neighbor dear to me.

I never hear his note in other places ;
But when June comes, and I return to live
Among the birches and memorial pines,
Lo, faithful to the tryst, alert and buoyant,
His strain familiar greets my welcoming soul,
And seems the type of all time-keeping things,
Rebuking chance and change.   Illusion sweet
Uprises with the sound : of all the birds

I know, this songster speaks most plain to me, *The Ground-Robin.*
Making impermanence a very myth.

So carol on, ground-robin ! each green year
I listen for you, and 'twould be a grief
Beyond mere words, some June, some fragrant
   morrow,
To sit and hearken by the open window
In vain ; for in a flood of fond regret
Would come a sense of loss, of unrequited
Love, of faith broken at length, of fickle
Friendship, and joy too beautiful to last :
        Sing on, ground-robin, sing !

FROM THE GRASS

NOW, for a moment, all is well :
   The eye looks out on lovely things —
Midsummer's facile miracle
Of sky and field and bird-swift wings.

Hush, heart, deep fellow feeling all
The world-pain ; haply this may be
A symbol of some good to fall,
Come homing-time, for me and thee.

The old illusion ?   Nature's art
To cozen us of Life's keen smart ?
Nay, life is love ; love lasts, O heart.

LOVE IS STRONG

A VIEWLESS thing is the wind,
But its strength is mightier far
Than a phalanxed host in battle line,
Than the limbs of a Samson are.

And a viewless thing is Love,
And a name that vanisheth;
But her strength is the wind's wild strength above,
For she conquers shame and Death.

CLAIRVOYANCE

THE worldling sat and cursed his empty fate,
His haggard, hopeless days, the cruelty
Practised upon his fellow-men by powers
Pitiless, inscrutable.   And then he turned
And saw beside him sit the quiet nun
In garb of meek-worn black touched soft with
white
About the neck, and from a purple string
Pendent the Christ upon a cross of bronze.
His fevered pulses cooled and calmed before
Those faithful eyes, the peace across the brow,
The pallor of long vigils and the joy
Of sacrifice, that made a lambency
Of the plain features.
                                    Of a sudden then
He knew his vision blurred, his bitterness
Misuse of dear-worth hours; what he called sight,
Purblindness of the flesh, now he beheld
The crystal-clear clairvoyance of the Pure.

MY UPPER SHELVES

CLOSE at my feet in stolid rows they sit,
The grave great tomes that furnish forth my
  wit ;
Like reverend oaks they are of Academe,
Within whose shade broods science, thought-
  adream.
I honor them and hearken to their lore,
And with a formal fondness view them o'er ;
As ever with the wise, they have the floor !

But high on top, all other books above,
The precious pocket volumes that I love
Forgather, in a Friends' Society
Whose silences are pregnant unto me.
The poets be there, companions tried and true
On many a walk, for many a fireside brew ;
The golden lays of Greece, the grace urbane
Of Roman Horace ; or some later strain
From lyre Elizabethan, passion-strong ;
From minnesinger or from master-song ;
And down the tuneful choirs of nearer days,
The chants of Hugo, or the soulful praise
Of Wordsworth, tranced among his native fells ;
The orphic art of Emerson ; the wail
Of Heine, ever slave to Beauty's spells ;
The voice of Tennyson in many a musing tale.
These and their fellows poise above my head,
And at their beck imperious I am led
Through all delights of living and of dead.

Less weighty, say you ?   All aërial things
That float on fancies or that fly on wings
Are small of bulk, and hence soar heaven-high ;
They have all manner of wild sweet escapes
From bonds of earth, and so they do not die
As die these grosser, more imprisoned shapes.
My upper shelves uphc d a mystic crowd,
Whose lightest word, though scarcely breathed
    aloud,
Will all outweigh a million folios
That groan with wisdom and with scholar-woes,
So long as love is love and blooms a sole red rose !

CONTRASTS

STRANGE, that we creatures of the petty
ways,
Poor prisoners behind these fleshly bars,
Can sometimes think us thoughts with God
    ablaze,
Touching the fringes of the outer stars.

And stranger still that, having flown so high
    And stood unshamed in shining presences,
We can resume our smallness, nor imply
    In mien or gesture what that memory is.

DAY AND NIGHT MUSIC

THE multitudinous murmurings of Day !
    The jocund motions that are in the trees,
The flecks of sunshine tossing in the breeze,
The meadow music that is miles away,

The volant birds that cannot stay from song,
The sound of woods and waters, spirits strong, —
      These, all of these,
Are of the light, and to the Day belong.

Nor less, the populous breathings of the Night :
The vast and vocal rhythms far and near
Of the cicadas, and the tree-toads' clear
Exalted answer from their leafy height ;
The bats that haunt the air with dusky whir,
The myriad nameless things that are astir, —
      These all appear
As myrmidons of Night and parts of her.

CLOWN AND KING

HOOP–LA, hey ! cried the clown in the ring,
   (Weep, weep, said his heart).
Alack a-day ! sighed the stately king,
    (Leap, leap, said his heart).

The clown's dear daughter lay a-dying,
And so his painted face was trying
    To veil an anguished mind.

The king's chief rival lay a-dying ;
His grief was mock, for he was trying
    To make the big world blind.

Whene'er I fear there is no God,
But blindest force in star and sod,
   A whisper says : There must be One
   To read beneath what things are done
    And grasp the doer's will ;

The clown's wrung heart,
The king's cold art,
Life's woven good-and-ill.

OF MUSIC

THE miner delves in caverns of the earth
Away from God's dear light, from everything
That breedeth joy and hope and wholesome mirth.
Ah, heaven, how fair the change, how good
to spring
Into the open, after dark and dearth !

The sailor gasps upon a sullen sea,
Shipwrecked, half mad for water, dying there ;
Yet all the brine is but a mockery,
And devils leer along the burning air.
Then, rain ! how all-divine that drink must be !

One, a world wanderer, drifts from strand to strand
For heedless years, — but then is fain to roam
No more ; he longs to clasp some kinsman's hand,
To sleep in sacred chambers of his home.
How blest the day he hails the loved, lost land !

But neither light, nor drink, nor home ways stir
Such rare delight, such infinite keen bliss
In them, as comes to me, a worshipper
Of music, when I hear it yearn and kiss :
Life thrills, grows luminous-large, smells sweet
with balm and myrrh.

GREAT AND SMALL

THE highest hills
   Are wrinkles in Time's transitory dust ;
The tiniest rills
Are seas at birth that mould the earth's huge crust ;
There is nor great nor small, — our fumbling eyes
Confuse the Essence with mere shape and size.

ANTICLIMAX

I WALKED a city street, and suddenly
   I saw a tiny lad.   The winter wind
Howled fitfully, and all the air above
The clear-cut outline of the buildings tall
Seemed full of knives that cut against the face :
An awful night among the unhoused poor !
The boy was tattered ; both his hands were thrust
For show of warmth within his pocket-holes,
Where pockets had not been for many a day.
One trouser-leg was long enough to hide
The naked flesh, but one, in mockery
A world too short, though he was monstrous small,
Left bare and red his knee — a cruel thing !
Then swelled my selfish heart with tenderness
And pity for the waif : to think of one
So young, so seeming helpless, homeless too,
Breasting the night, a-shiver with the cold !
Gaining a little, soon I passed him by,
My fingers reaching for a silver coin
To make him happier, if only for
An hour, when — I marvelled as I heard —
His mouth was puckered up in cheery wise,

And in the very teeth of fortune's frown
He whistled loud a scrap of some gay tune !
And I must know that all my ready tears
Fell on a mood more merry than mine own.

PERSONIFICATION

MAKE Him a name, a something vague, enskied,
    You win cool heads, perchance, to cool
  assent ;
Make Him a babe unwitting, open-eyed,
All mother hearts enclasp the Innocent ;
Make Him a man, careworn and crucified,
And straight men love Him, knowing what is
  meant.

WINTER TWILIGHT

A LITTLE while ago and you might see
  The ebon trees against the saffron sky
That shifts through flame to rose ; but now a calm
Of solemn blue above, a stilly time,
With pines that peer and listen, while the snow
Gleams ghostly and the brittle sound of ice
Tinkles along the dumbness, strangely loud,
Since all the air is tranced. Housed-in, the folk
Close-gather at the ingle, and the hour
Of fireside cheer and homely talk of kin
Is welcomed, as the big, vague world beyond
Moves nightward, merges into mystery.

44

THE RURAL PIPE

(THE RUSTIC POET SOLILOQUIZES)

NAY, chide me not because my pipe oft sings
Of country doings and of common things :

Of sun-steeped fields where men forestall the day
To gather up in mows the winter's hay ;

Of kine called musically at the bars,
And swaying home beneath the early stars ;

Of woods divinely cool, where moss and fern
Do haunt the pleasant places of the burn ;

Of berry pickings, and of harvest fun
Beneath the moon when day-work all is done ;

Of fall forgatherings, when nuts are thick,
And boys beat out the burrs with lusty stick ;

Of storm-bound labors and of snowings-in,
When water lacks, and low is every bin ;

Of cutting ice upon the waveless lake,
Where skaters whirl and frosty music make ;

Of these, and more, the happenings manifold,
Whereby the countryside's full tale is told.

Nay, chide me not, for these are things I see
And know and love — the very heart of me.

So did Theocritus, and still we hear
His airs Sicilian and his message clear.

THE RAIN ON THE ROOF

UNDER the eaves is the haunt I love !
  With the outer world a myth,
With the cloud-sea drowning the stars above,
  And the day work over with ;
To lean me back with my thoughts in tune,
  To feel from my cares aloof,
To hear o'erhead in a soothing rune
    The rain on the roof.

'Tis a magic realm, where I am king ;
  I can live a whole life through
In a transient hour, and my dreamings bring
  Delight that is ever new ;
And the cries without of the weather wild
  Seem all for my sole behoof ;
And it makes my heart the heart of a child,
    The rain on the roof.

My wonder-book it is nigh at hand,
  The drip-drip lulls me to rest ;
'Tis a music soft and a spirit bland,
  And a comrade whose way is best.
So I see but the fair, smooth face of Life,
  Forgetting its cloven hoof,
As I lie and list to the wind's wild strife,
    The rain on the roof.

For old-time voices and boyhood calls,
  Laughter silver and tears,
All float in as the evening falls
  And summons the vanished years.

Though the warp be sombre that binds me round, *The Rain*
   Yet a sweet and shining woof *on the*
Is woven in with that winsome sound, *Roof.*
     The rain on the roof.

A MYSTERY

WHY should a fir-tree stark against the sky
   Arouse old thoughts and times of long ago ;
Yea, blind with tears a careless passing eye
   That chancewise looks for signs of rain or snow ?
     I do not know,

I only feel that any joy or pain
   May live afresh in any sight I see,
By field or nook, by path or windy plain.
   And so the world a wonder is to me,
     A mystery.

TO A MOUNTAIN BROOK

BEAUTY and health do companion thee,
  friend,
   Boons evanescent and rare ;
Daytime and night-tide in loveliness bend
   Over thy flight that is fair.

Rarer boon still : It is given to thee —
   Far from the fret that is mine —
To hark thine own music, and know it to be
   Born of an impulse divine.

DEMOCRACY

KINGDOMS and crowns have been from
storied years ;
But older, sager, that Democracy
As wide as life, as sure as human tears
And smiles, that ever is and e'er must be.

Our great Republic of the common woe,
The common joy ; no marks nor metes of man
Confine its borders, and no rivers flow
Splitting its people into tribe and clan.

One nation, breathing in the selfsame air,
All freedmen in the privilege of pain ;
Each soul holds franchise in the right to dare
The altitudes, to fall, and dare again.

LYRIC AND EPIC

A LITTLE lyric the sunset gleamed
At eve, a heart-song warm with love,
Light-drenched gold, and a pink that dreamed ;
Shot with life and the sweet thereof,
Yet inly, deeply calm it seemed.

At morn an epic filled the eye,
Moving grand with a hero's gait ;
Rain that raged in a wide, gray sky,
Winds that moaned disconsolate,
An elemental clash and cry.

ON A FERRY–BOAT

THE river widens to a pathless sea
  Beneath the rain and mist and sullen skies.
Look out the window ; 'tis a gray emprise,
This piloting of massed humanity
  Onsuch a day, from shore to busy shore,
  And breeds the thought that beauty is no more.

But see yon woman in the cabin seat,
  The Southland in her face and foreign dress ;
  She bends above a babe, with tenderness
That mothers use ; her mouth grows soft and
    sweet.
  Then, lifting eyes, ye saints in heaven, what
    pain
  In that strange look of hers into the rain !

There lies a vivid band of scarlet red
  With careless grace across her raven hair ;
  Her cheek burns brown ; and 'tis her way to
    wear
A gown where colors stand in satin's stead.
  Her eye gleams dark as any you may see
  Along the winding roads of Italy.

What dreamings must be hers of sunny climes,
  This beggar woman midst the draggled throng !
  How must she pine for solaces of song,
For warmth and love to furnish laughing-times !
  Her every glance upon the waters gray
  Is piteous with some lost yesterday.

49

I've seen a dove, storm-beaten, far at sea ;
   And once a flower growing stark alone
   From out a rock ; I've heard a hound make
     moan
Left masterless : but never came to me
   Ere this such sense of creatures torn apart
   From all that fondles life and feeds the heart.

RECOLLECTIONS

I SEE a lad deserted by his mates,
   Because his ways were little to their mind,
   Turn sick at heart, shed tears to make him
     blind ;
So sad, that never have the after-fates
Brought pain that pinched more close, a day more
     dark,
Though many since have sullen been and stark ;
   And yet we call our childhood soft and kind !

Again I see him, stretched along the floor,
   Reading with bated breath and blue eyes keen
   Of her the mystic maiden called Undine ;
Of how she won a knight beside the shore,
With looks that stirred his heart to nameless fears.
The reader burst into a storm of tears
   That day she sank beneath the waters green.

Now, older grown, but still a very lad,
   He stands beside a woman, strokes her hair
   And touches timidly the love-locks there,
Laying his soul before her beauty glad,

Though she be twice his years.   He draws his
  breath
More worshipfully than to his hour of death
  He will again — a lad's first love is fair!

One night, he lies abed in wakefulness,
  The while his mother plays and sings below
  Some dim sweet melody of long ago,
And sad withal, beyond his saddest guess ;
Until the childish heart swells big with pain.
Through all the years it sounds for him again,
  That mother's voice, that music sobbing so !

And last, one day stands out from those gone by,
  And those that followed, as a single tree
  Stands out, a creature lonesome utterly,
Upon a desert 'gainst a flaming sky.
'Twas when his father died ; he made no sound,
But in a secret place upon the ground
  They found him — dazed and dumb that such
    could be.

Ah, recollections, how ye throng and set
  Time's dial back, until the by-gones teem
  With potent doings ! How the child-days seem
As dewy as a spring-time violet,
Sad as the flower, too, when night-tide comes,
Yet sweet with all the sweets her bosom sums ;
  Yea, bitter sweet — a message and a dream !

51

AS A VIOLINIST

AS a violinist bends a loving face
Down to his fiddle, down to the singing
bow,
So the poet bends down his soul to Beauty's place
For to hear her voice, and her very heart to know.
As the player looks aloft and thrills the strings,
So the poet looks to God, and yearns and sings.

TRAGI–COMEDY

I SIT a mute spectator in the pit,
And watch the tragi-comedy of Life :
The buffoon's laughter, and the flash of wit,
The love that leavens, and the assassin's knife.

And just because an act is yet to come
(The fifth, that evens all, and dries our tears),
My foolish thoughts are dark and troublesome,
And over-sad the tangled plot appears.

But if I still remain, as others do,
Trusting the playwright, sitting with my
friends,
Methinks the story will prove sweet and true,
And I shall read its meaning as it ends.

THE MARSH FLOWER

DOWN in a marsh by the water's brink
I found a bloom of the palest pink ;
And I watched it oft and loved it well,
For it touched my heart with a mystic spell.

Till at last I plucked the flower fair
And bore it home, and summoned there
A friend, to give me its proper name,
Its habitat and its right to fame.

And he told me then.   But it sounded harsh ;
In my ignorance by the lonesome marsh
I had called it *Child-of-my-Soul,* and smiled
To think of its beauty growing wild.

And he told me more ; but every word
Was wisdom such as I wished unheard.
And lo ! when the story all was said,
The bloom in my hand lay shrunk and dead.

SAINTHOOD

AN angel came and plead with tuneful voice
Before a maiden fair in youth's demesne :
" Now, daughter, seize the right and make your
    choice
Of God forever, spotless to be seen.

" So shall you live your life, and die in peace,
    And as the years flit by in noiseless flight,
You shall be sainted, and your name increase,
    Your deeds be inspirations day and night."

The maiden kneeled, awe written on her face,
    And said : " Ah, holy spirit, how can I
That am not fair, that have no touch of grace,
    That am as other maidens dwelling by,

53

Sainthood. " Be like to those great pictures that I see
        Of saints long worshipped, wrapt in sinless rest ?
Dear angel, surely such is far from me ;
        Dear angel, show me how I may be blest.''

Then smiled the spirit : " Daughter, trust my
        word ;
    You cannot see how such a sainthood came.
Nor can you measure how men's souls are stirred,
    Nor how old Time makes magic of a name.

" Live out your maiden life, I tell you now,
    And it will all suffice, great deeds apart :
For just a smile and just a tender brow
    Are sainted by the hungry, human heart.''

AN AUTUMN IMPRESSION

A FROST came over night. Then all the day
    The leaves fell groundward, fluttered down
in shoals,
With sound of sober music, from the trees,
Until foot-farers ploughed through russet waves
That rustled crisply, fresh with scents of earth ;
All day the air was yellow with the flight.
The sun at noon was mystic-large and seemed
To faint in smoke, — but when it sank and set
It left the West a miracle, a place
Where sombre autumn tints waked suddenly
Into an ecstasy of vivid lights
And trembling fires, that passed to mortal calms.

54

Then came the eve and with her lovely eyes
Soothed all the sunset passion, made the sky
A haunt for spirits and a home for stars.

CHARITY

PORTIA with silver tongue hath spoken of
The quality of mercy, long ago ;
There is no human thing more deep than love ;
Ask any soul and it shall tell you so.

And Paul, large-hearted, spake with golden words
And said the same, foreseeing days to be,
His speech more sweet than any sound of birds :
" The greatest of these all is Charity."

STREAM AND SINGER

THE stream has a steady voice,
And some will listen and say :
" Ah ! look how her waves rejoice,
A-leap through the night and day."
But bend you close, if you may,
And soon you will feel and know
How her cry is a sorrow-throe
That yearns for the far away.

The singer is glad betimes,
But his under-thought is a tear.
He will ripple along in rhymes
That speak of the springing year ;
But stand you beside, and hear
The beat of his heart, and soon

There will sound a sob in the tune
That is full of the dim and dear.

But the sorrow is ne'er for naught
Of the stream and the poet's cry,
For they tell of a treasure sought,
And they moan that it is not nigh ;
Till the folk who are passing by
Are moved with a deep desire
To strive and to still aspire,
Though the dawns and the day-tides die.

CRICKETS

I HEARD the crickets on the summer hills,
The wights whose shrill and intermittent voice,
In multitudinous chorus, makes the day
Seem interplight with ceaseless sound, the night
A sleep-begetting time, because their cry
Is constant still.   And then I thought, how soon
The autumn's breath would blow and blight their
    cheer,
And sift above the grass the heartless snow
Of winter, while the bleak wind howled a jest
Above those minstrels buried in their prime.
And then I longed to know if, one and all,
These little bards, so strenuous in their chant,
Could look beyond December e'en to May,
E'en to another year at summer-tide,
When once again the hills should vocal be

With their swart brotherhood — could compass this *Crickets.*
Prophetic hope, and so take heart of grace
To shrill and fill the air and pleasure me,
Until I loved them and their quest of song.

SEA WITCHERY

YON headland, with the twinkling footed sea
Beyond it, conjures shapes and stories fair
Of young Greek days : the lithe immortal air
Carries the sound of Siren-song to me ;
Soon shall I mark Ulysses daringly
Swing round the cape, the sea-wind in his hair :
And look ! The Argonauts go sailing there
A golden quest, shouting their god-like glee.
The vision is compact of blue and gold,
Of sky and water, and the drift of foam,
And thrill of brine-washed breezes from the west :
Wide space is in it, and the unexpressed
Great heart of Nature, and the magic old
Of legend, and the white ships coming home.

IN A LIBRARY

A WEALTH of silence, that is all.   The air
Lacks life and holds no hint of tender spring,
Of flowers wholesome-blowing, birds a-wing,
Of any creature much alive and fair.
Perchance you guess a murmur here and there
Among the tomes, each book a gossip thing,
And each in her own tongue — yet slumbering
Seems more the bookish fashion everywhere.

But ah, could but the souls take flesh again
That wrought these words, their hearts all passion-
    swirled,
What companies would flock and fill the stage,
Resuming now their old imperious reign !
Knight, noble lady, priest, the saint and sage,
The valor, bloom, and wisdom of a world.

BROOKLYN BRIDGE

I READ of marvels in removed lands,
  Of old fabricians deft, of structures vast :
  The world knew seven wonders in the past,
And all upreared by cunning mortal hands.
But he who on this mighty creature stands
    And sees the sun strike spire and dome and mast,
    Awe-struck, must say : This shall them all out-
      last,
Imperishable above time's shifting sands.

But nay, all works of human-kind wax old,
  And e'en the stars we call eternal shine
Less strong and die ; men pass beneath the sod ;
  All things are transient as the joys of wine ;
Save that through all, the drifting years behold
  One changeless purpose in the mind of God.

A PALIMPSEST

I GAZE along the frore, dim fields, and, lo !
  By dint of gazing, or by witchery
Beyond my ken, I sudden seem to see
The Summer, odorous, warm, and all aglow
With bounties of the earth, with skies that glow

In beauty with the day.   There floats to me *A*
    The tinkle of the sheep-bells on the lea,   *Palimpsest.*
The plaining of the brook, the tree-tops' low
And sibilant song.   The Winter is effaced,—
    That was the writing of a later hand,
A gloomy screed ; and now mine eyes have traced
    The early, joyous message of the land
When life was rife with roses east and west —
Have read the secret of God's palimpsest.

FROM A CITY WINDOW

AFTER a breathing space in quiet nooks,
    Sweet days of fellowship with Spring and
  Sun,
Midst buds half blown, midst bird songs just begun,
Midst greening meadows and rain-swollen brooks,
How soiled and roiled the seething city looks ! —
Its roar of trade, its feverish tides that run
Through channels choked, —its legends, one by
    one,
Of fates more strange than those in wonder-books !

And yet I feel a throb exultant, strong,
About to breast this hoarse, tumultuous sea :
" Ah, here is Life," I say beneath my breath ;
" Here all ambitions jostle fitfully,
Here saints and sinners mingle, sob and song,
While far removed seems any thought of Death."

REMEMBERED SONGS

I WALKED an autumn lane, and ne'er a tune
  Besieged mine ear from hedge or ground or
  tree ;
The summer minstrels all had fared from me
Far Southward, since the snows must flock so soon.
And yet the air seemed vibrant with the croon
Of unseen birds and words of Maytide glee :
The very silence was a melody
Sown thick with memoried cadences of June.

Shall we not hold that when our little day
Is done, and we are seen of men no more,
We still live on in some such subtile way,
To make some silence vocal by some shore
Of Recollection, or to inly play
Soft songs on hearts that loved us, long before ?

COLUMBUS

I SEE a caravel of Spanish make
  That westward like a wingéd creature flies
Above a sea dawn-bright, and arched with skies
Expectant of the sun and morning-break.
The sailors from the deck their land-thirst slake
With peering o'er the waves, until their eyes
Discern a coast that faint and dream-like lies,
The while they pray, weep, laugh, — or madly
  take
Their shipmates in their arms and speak no word.

And then I see a figure, tall, removed   *Columbus.*
A little from the others, as behooved,
That since the dawn has neither spoke nor stirred ;
A noble form the looming mast beside,
Columbus, calm, his prescience verified.

BEAUTY STILL WAITS

THE blent delight of summer !   Far and faint
   The hills, hard by the hayfield's fragrancy,
And yonder bosky thicket whence to me
Floated last night the thrush's mellow plaint,
Fit sound to woo the moon.   No cloud-flecks
   taint
The crystal sky that is so calm to see ;
The hey-day of the birds is come, the glee
Of brooks is heard ; each tree stands like a saint
In chastened meditation.   When the bard
Birth-claimed of seven cities oped his eyes
(Not blind as yet) upon a world more young,
Naught was more lovely.   Here in fairest guise
Beauty still waits upon the golden tongue
To show her forth, for man's most fond regard.

THE SOUL'S HOURS

BETIMES I steal to some sequestered place,
   Some seldom-travelled spot by wood or lane,
Or where the waters lift and lapse again
At the moon's summons.   There I turn my face
Up to the sun or stars, while visions trace

Their fawn-fleet way within my brooding brain,
And my sick soul that dormant long has lain
Takes deep delight in winds, and ample space.
Men deem me drowsed in slothful revery :
Not so : these be the sane and sacred hours
When most I feel Life's duty, joy, and loss.
Joy, for I rest amid unsullied flowers,
Duty as well, for in the heavens I see
Some cloud-formed adumbration of a Cross.

ACROSS THE INTERVALE

ALONG Life's lowlands, petty men
Mix in a crowd with thoughts earth-tied
And sympathies too narrow-eyed
To peer beyond their little Then.
They walk their ways, all unaware
Of folk-moots in the upper air.

But, few and far between, arise
Great souls who overtop the small
And local, who have range of all
The inspirations of the skies ;
Then each to each they cry *Good hail,*
Like peaks across an intervale.

HARMONY

A STILL, ineffable harmony
Unites to-day the land and sea ;
Their colors blend, their mood is one,
Upon them both the morning sun
Makes magic, potent-strong to me.

May Life, that soon is overpast,   *Harmony.*
Merge in Eternity's dim Vast
   With this same harmony, this sense
   Of beauty under difference ;
This brotherhood of First and Last.

A PRAYER

" In that day when I make up My jewels."

IN that fair day and dawn divine
   That sees Thy crown complete,
When radiant ones around Thee shine,
   And angels kiss Thy feet,

Dear Lord, may she, my little one,
   Among Thy jewels be :   ‹
Not flashing like a central sun,
   Not bold in brilliancy ;

But white, and modest, as beseems
   A meek and simple girl —
For I behold her in my dreams
   A small yet perfect pearl.

IN THE EAST

YOU say the foliage is rich and strange,
   The houses quaint, the palms and temple-domes
Bespeak another world — another range
   Of hopes and fears within these Orient homes.

And yet, I swear, the thought that pierces me
   Is not the new, the unfamiliar look ;
But rather do I marvel it can be
   So like the homeland that we have forsook.

For over all the sky is calm and gray,
   An old-time friend ; and all the men I meet
Look forth from human eyes, and seem to say
   Hail, brother ! as they pass along the street.

DISSONANCES

OFT in the midst of music rare
Comes a break in the fluent air ;

Seeming dissonances creep
Into the chords once tender, deep.

But, as the deft musician plays
On to the end, the music strays

Back to harmonies that are meet,
Making the whole a thing more sweet.

So, from the strings of the harp of life
Notes may be struck with discord rife ;

But when the air is played, you see
They were a part of the melody.

BETWEEN THE SUNS

ENGLOOMED between the cosmic flare of
suns,
There are vast spaces, cold and pitiless,
Where nothing save an awful atom-dance
Bespeaks of life.   Yet will that taper wee,

64

That peering little light called Faith, essay
To pierce this night of eons, and declare
Each atom, every inch of whirling void,
Vital, yea, kind and luminous with God.

THE PINES

THE pines are solemn souls, now brooding o'er
Their reverend past ; now filled with bodeful
dreams
Of their dim future, with its sorry change
From long-while sequestration (peering up
Into a sky of peace, and rooted fast
In mother earth) to restless voyaging,
To dumb unease above the shifty sea,
As masts that men have fashioned ; to a fate
That bids them wander, ne'er to find a home.

MY POETS

I SAW them in my dreams, — a goodly band
With lyre of gracious make within each hand,
A laurel wreath upon each shining head,
All young as youth and all fair-garmented.

They swept the strings beside a magic sea
That ever beat its waves in melody
Upon a shore where blooms immortal sprang
Between their feet, for solace while they sang.

I waked, and saw them in the light of day :
A motley crowd, for some were bent and gray,
And some clothed on with rags and hollow-eyed,
And others limped, as they had journeyed wide.

My Poets. And oftenwhiles they sang when racked with pain,
　　　Or spake of field and flower, of Love's domain,
　　　　When mured about by sad and noisome sights
　　　　And lacking air and space and May delights.

　　　And yet methinks I loved their motley more
　　　Than those dream-singers that I saw before ;
　　　　And yet methinks they looked of heavenly race
　　　　By some strange token on their brow and face !

TWO MOTHERS

A WOMAN walking the street adown
　　Saw at a casement glint the gown
Of a mother, meek, whose little son
Had died with his child-joys just begun.
And it smote her heart, for well she knew
What mother-love with a life may do ;
And she said, " Poor soul ! how sad that she
Should lose the child in his grace and glee ! "
For she thought of *her* boy that lived to-day,
Though man-grown now and far away.

But the woman there in the window-seat
Looked with a smile, not sad, but sweet,
And touched with pity, to the place
Where she had marked the other's face ;
And she said, " Poor soul ! her child is lost,
For now he is only a man sin-tossed !
But the boy I watched in his bright young day,
He bides in my heart a child for aye."

SEA AND SHORE

HAVE you marked how the sea with foam
   At the kiss of the shore turns white ?
She has found a love and a home ;
   Then why should she lack delight ?

A thought lies cold at her heart,
   Till she pales all suddenly ;
For she knows they must part, must part,
   When the tide sets out to sea.

USES

SWEET smells upsteal from the ground
            After the rain ;
      Sweet thoughts in the soul are found
            After long pain.

      Rain, with its dark and wet,
            Fathers the flowers ;
      Pain, on a mortal set,
            Saddens the hours,

      Only to gladder go
            After a span.
      Rain for the rose, I trow,
            Tears for man.

A SEASCAPE OF TURNER'S

I SEE the gulls and I smell the main,
   The wind goes shrieking shrilly by ;
   With cordage-creak and canvas-strain
   The good ship heaves to meet the sky.

'Tis wild and wet on the waters now,
The oars must bend ere they reach the land ;
Yon man that makes alive the bow,
His face means, *Home and my baby's hand.*

Ah, brave to show us, within four walls,
The Pulse o' the sea, her angry might !
Ah, brave to show us how deep love calls
Across the waves like a harbor-light !

PERMANENCY

A LOVER carved upon a bed of stone
His lady's name, and set thereto a rhyme ;
And on the rock were marks beside his own,
Scratched by a glacier in primeval time.

And yet the passion that his spirit stirred,
The while he cut her fond and fleeting name,
Methinks was more eternal than the word
The ice age spoke — time's snow against love's
flame !

ON SYRIAN HILLS

IT is said the Bedouins cry, on the Syrian hills,
a clear
Loud summons to War, and the tribes far
distant hearken and hear,
So wondrous rare is the air, so crystal the atmosphere.

Their call is to arms ; but One, in the centuries *On*
   long ago,   *Syrian*
Spake there for Peace, in tones that were marvel- *Hills.*
   lous sweet and low,
And the ages they hear Him yet, and His voice do
   the nations know.

PERSONALITY

IF I heard a voice in the upper air
That sounded heavenly sweet and fair,
'Twould gladden me, my life would take
A sudden leap for the music's sake.

But gladlier far, O sweet, I stay
Beside you here as you sit and play
Soft dreamy things in the minor keys,
Or major parts with their harmonies.

For love is love, and soul seeks soul
In the minor's sob or the major's roll ;
And I know that back of the chords divine
Are the hand and the beating heart of thine !

THE PRAYERS OF SAINTS

Golden vials full of odors, which are the prayers of saints. —
REV. v : 8.

NO fragrance of the early months, when
earth
Teems with the pledge of after-blossoming,
No May day scents of bud and leaf, no morn
Of June rose-regal — none of these have worth

For sweetness of the savor they do bring
Compared with that rich incense swift upborne
By saintly prayers unto God's very face —
Soul emanations, odors mixed with grace,
Perfumed and perfect for that heavenly place.

TREES IN WINTER

THROUGH a dumb-shifting veil of snow
I mark the trees. The chestnuts bare,
That reach black fingers up the air ;
The beeches where, high branch and low,

The leaves still hang in russet ranks ;
The oaks, whose leaves are scanter, more
Phantasmal-brown, mere ghosts of yore ;
The elms, of shapelier tops and flanks.

And then the pines : sole guests in green
The summer does vouchsafe ; they stand
Sedately, dropping from their hand
The pungent cones ; dark, dark, I ween,

Their thoughts, and deep and manifold.
The winter grass seems doubly sere
Beneath their vital boughs that fear
No frost, that changeless front the cold.

These stately creatures all I view
As through an opal dimly ; then,
Illimitable, mute to men,
Above, a sky of hodden gray

That stretches on to that Somewhere
Which bounds my ultimate land of dreams,
Wherein the Ideal lures and gleams,
Wherein the soul breathes native air.

THE PATH

FAR, far I've strayed me in the long endeavor
    To find the way of Truth ;
All unfamiliar grow the paths, and ever
        I lose the step of youth,

Until it seems I am foredoomed to wander
        In fruitless, weary quest,
While strength and time and hope I do but
        squander,
        Seeking the final rest.

Sometimes poor mortals, forest-bound, have
        plodded
        Along an unblazed trail,
And felt strange fears and seen weird shapes em-
        bodied,
        That made their courage fail ;

Then suddenly have found they circled blindly,
        And were not far astray,
Led by some hand invisible but kindly
        Into a wonted way.

So, haply, I, sore spent with ceaseless trying,
        Too tired to longer roam,
May sudden see the path before me lying,
        And just ahead my home.

A ROYAL PROGRESS

THE Summer is a queen who proudly makes
    A Royal Progress through the subject land :
Whereat a festal look the highway takes,
And e'en the byways, too, on every hand
Turn gay with buds and birds and bloomy trees,
The gracious Lady Sovereign for to please.

EPITAPH OF AN ACTOR

HERE lies a servant of the mimic art ;
    He pictured Life, its passion and its glee.
Death bade him play, at last, a grim-faced part,
His only make-up, man's mortality.

RECOMPENSE

FOR every man that dies, some little one
    Is born, they say, into this world of ours ;
I wonder if, for every evil done,
    Some deed unfolds fair-hearted, like the flowers ?

RICHARD WAGNER

OLD deeds, old creeds, for centuries dead,
    rise out
The grave and swarm beside the storied Rhine :
The thunders of the heaven are girt about
    With silver zones of melody divine.

SUNRISE

THE broadening of the light is like a strain
Of mellow music from a golden horn
  Set to the huntsman's lips, who now is fain
To play *hunt's up*, and wake the drowsy morn.

RAIN AND SLEEP

IT is no marvel that the morn is fair
And fresh, that Nature's mood is blithe again ;
For all the night these blessed her unaware :
  The balm of sleep, the baptism of rain.

TRANSFORMATION

THE butterflies are buttercups, wind-blown,
  Bright, airy flowers upon the summer's
  breast ;
The buttercups, thick in the meadows sown,
Are butterflies flight-weary, seeking rest.

www.ingramcontent.com/pod-product-compliance
Lightning Source LLC
Chambersburg PA
CBHW021427090426
42742CB00009B/1291